VISIONS OF

SPORT

The World's Greatest Sports Photography

gettyimages®

VSP

INTRODUCTION

Visions of Sport is not a book of photographs of iconic sporting moments, although you will see many such images scattered throughout the book, from heavyweight boxing legend Muhammad Ali's 'phantom punch' knockout of Sonny Liston in 1965 to sprinter Usain Bolt's world-record-obliterating heroics at the 2008 Olympics. Neither is it a book of pictures of iconic players, despite many legendary figures from the world of sport featuring on the following pages, from Bob Beamon to Sachin Tendulkar. Rather it is a collection of exceptional photographs capturing sport in all its diversity – triumph, defeat, technique, bravery, passion, breathtaking skill, speed, moments of stillness, colour, quirkiness, concentration, physical agility, mental cruelty, teamwork, single-mindedness.

The 156 stunning pictures presented in this book were selected from the 12 million sports photographs (and counting) stored in the archives of Getty Images, one of the world's leading photographic and multimedia agencies. With such a wealth of outstanding photographs at our disposal, the editing process was necessarily brutal. Some exceptional sportsmen and women did not make the cut. Our selection criteria throughout the book, including the 52-page Olympic games section, was quite simple: is this a great photograph?

Whether it is an image of footballer Wayne Rooney perfectly executing an overhead kick to score the goal of the 2010/11 Premier League season, a Japanese university student on the receiving end of a sly punch during a not-so-friendly rugby match, or an unidentified Olympic kayak rower in early-morning practice, silhouetted against the rising sun, it has been included in this book on its merits as a photograph. Consequently, the photographer is credited alongside each picture wherever their name is known, because it is their skill, perception and planning – allied, sometimes, to a bit of luck – that has created such spectacular images as much as the endeavours of their subjects. This book brings together their outstanding work to create a visual feast which is sure to wow any lover of sport and high-end photography.

Opposite page Andres Iniesta of Spain celebrates Spain's 1-0 triumph over the Netherlands at the final whistle of the FIFA World Cup final at Soccer City Stadium in Johannesburg, South Africa on July 11, 2010.
Photo by Alex Livesey/FIFA/Getty Images

Right Paulie Malignaggi feels
Amir Khan's power during
their WBA Light Welterweight
World Championship boxing
match at Madison Square
Garden in New York City,
May 15, 2011.
*Photo by John Gichigi/
Getty Images*

Above Sun worshippers are oblivious to the efforts of British driver Jenson Button during practice for the Monaco Formula One Grand Prix, May 22, 2008.
Photo by Paul Gilham/Getty Images

Opposite page A painter takes a break to watch the peloton pass through the village of Sheriffhales on stage four of the Tour of Britain from Wolverhampton to Birmingham, September 1, 2006.
Photo by Julian Finney/Getty Images

Opposite page The Great Britain synchronised swimming team perform their technical routine during the European Swimming Championship in Budapest, Hungary, August 6, 2010.
Photo by Clive Rose/
Getty Images

Left Athletes compete in the mixed relay discipline during the 2011 IBU Biathlon World Championship staged in Khanty-Mansiysk, Russia, March 3, 2011.
Photo by Alexander
Hassenstein/Bongarts/
Getty Images

Left Pittsburgh Pirates' fans atop the University's Cathedral of Learning look down at Forbes Field and celebrate their team winning the 1960 World Series against New York Yankees.
Photo by George Silk/Time Life Pictures/ Getty Images

Below England manager Fabio Capello before a friendly match against Denmark at Parken Stadium in Copenhagen, February 9, 2011.
Photo by Michael Regan/Getty Images

Below right Future heavyweight boxing legend, Cassius Clay (later Muhammad Ali), lying on his hotel bed in London, holds up five fingers in a prediction of how many rounds it will take him to knock out Henry Cooper, May 27, 1963.
Photo by Len Trievnor/Express/Getty Images

Below BMW-Sauber driver Robert Kubica of Poland crashes during the Canadian Formula One Grand Prix at the Circuit Gilles Villeneuve in Montreal, June 10, 2007.
Photo by Paul Gilham/Getty Images

Right Made In Taipan, ridden by Robbie Power, clears the last fence during the Melling Steeplechase on Ladies' Day at Aintree, Liverpool, England, on April 8, 2011.
Photo by Alex Livesey/Getty Images

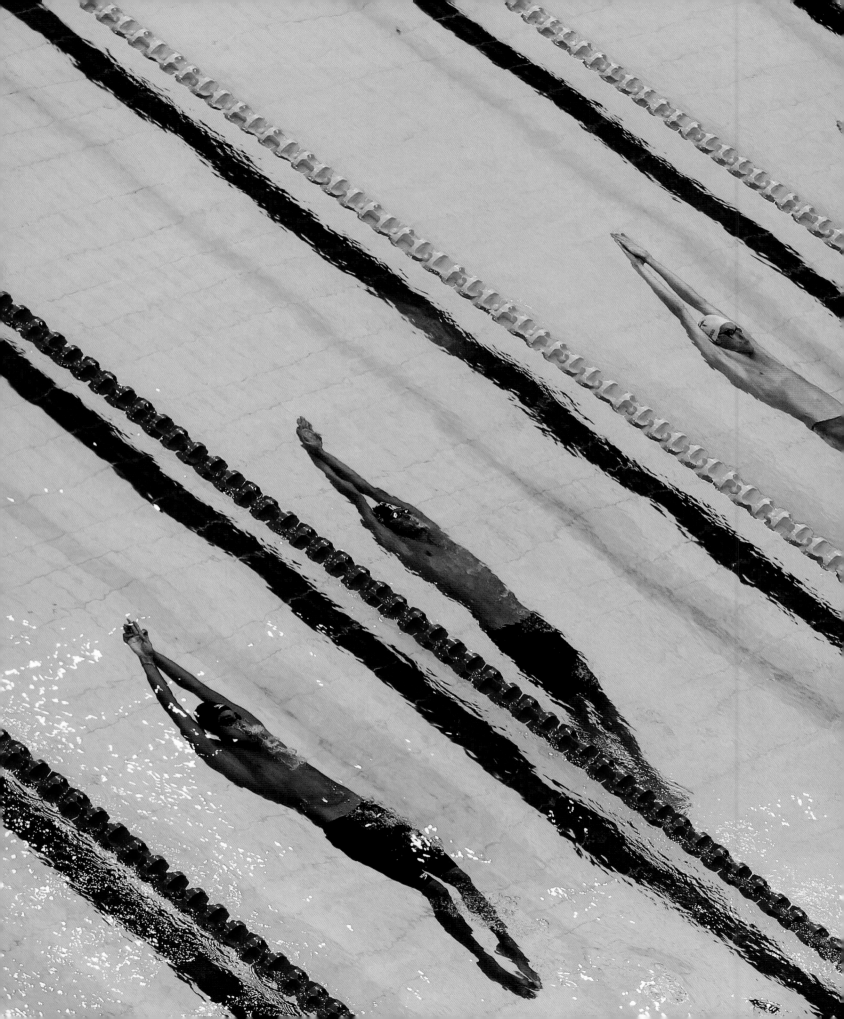

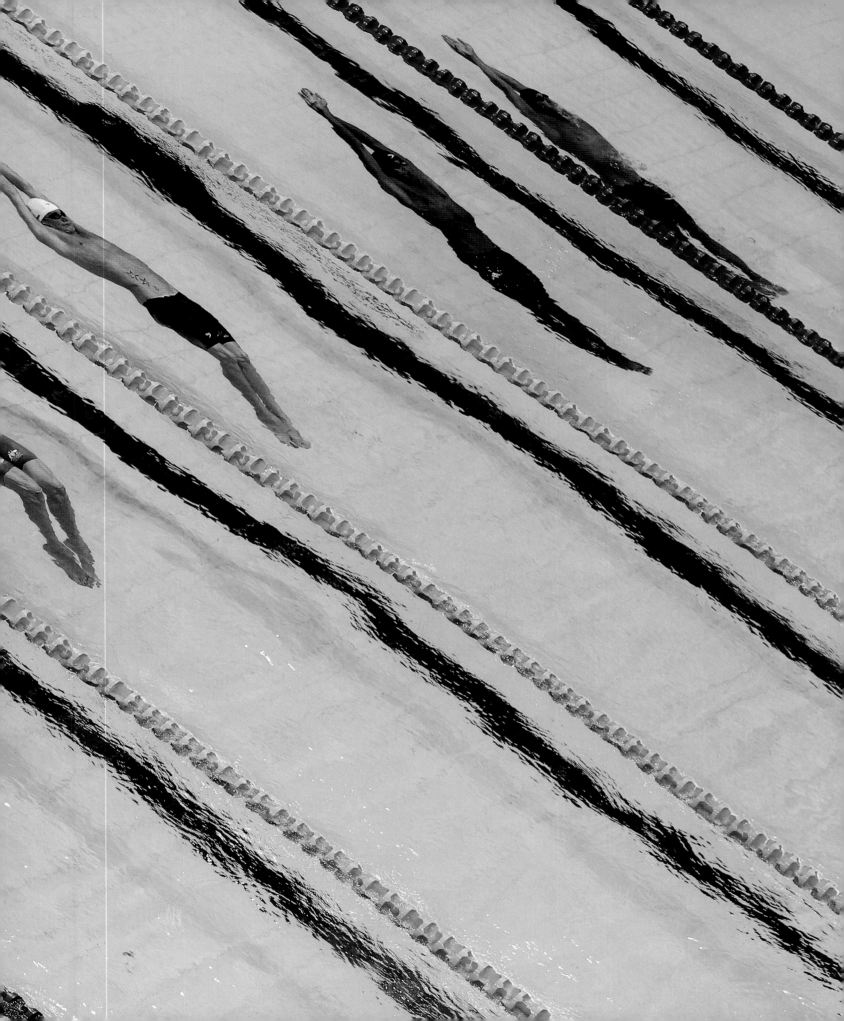

Above Kim Clijsters throws her racket during her match
against Alisa Kleybanova on day five of the 2011
Medibank International tournament at Sydney Olympic
Park Tennis Centre, Australia, January 13, 2011.
Photo by Mark Nolan/Getty Images

Opposite page Austria's Thomas Morgenstern of Austria
flies through the trial round for the FIS Ski Jumping World
Cup event of the 59th Four Hills Ski Jumping tournament
at Bergisel, Innsbruck, Austria, January 3, 2011.
Photo by Alex Grimm/Bongarts/Getty Images

Opposite page A not-so-friendly match between hosts Cambridge University and the Japanese University of Doshiba in 1989 sees Atsushi Ogagi of Japan take a hit in the line out.
Photo by Simon Bruty /Allsport

Above Nigel De Jong of the Netherlands 'tackles' Spain's Xabi Alonso in the World Cup final at Soccer City Stadium, Johannesburg, South Africa, July 11, 2010.
Photo by Mike Hewitt/Getty Images

Left Ayrton Senna waits in the McLaren team garage during practice for the Brazilian Grand Prix at the Jacarepagua circuit near Rio de Janeiro, Brazil, April 2, 1988.
Photo by Simon Bruty/ Getty Images

Above Champagne flows in the Red Bull Racing team garage at the Yas Marina Circuit in Abu Dhabi, after Sebastian Vettel clinches the Formula One Drivers' Championship, November 14, 2010.
Photo by Mark Thompson/Getty Images

Opposite page Sebastian Vettel driving through the rain on his way to winning the Chinese Formula One Grand Prix in Shanghai, April 19, 2009.
Photo by Clive Mason/Getty Images

Following pages LeBron James of the Miami Heat makes a dunk shot late in the fourth quarter during Game Five of the Eastern Conference semi-finals of the NBA Playoffs against the Boston Celtics, Miami, Florida, May 11, 2011.
Photo by Mike Ehrmann/Getty Images

Above Jose-Maria Olazabal leans on Seve Ballesteros during the 1991 Ryder Cup staged at Kiawah Island, South Carolina, USA.
Photo by David Cannon/Getty Images

Above right Middlesex batsman Mike Brearley and Yorkshire wicketkeeper David Bairstow, Lord's cricket ground, London, England, June 1980.
Photo by Adrian Murrell/Getty Images

Left Chris Yarran (top) of the Carlton Blues spoils the marking attempt of Collingwood Blues' Travis Cloke during an AFL match at Melbourne Cricket Ground, Australia, July 16, 2011.
Photo by Hamish Blair/Getty Images

Above Thierry Henry in midair at the City of Manchester Stadium, September 25, 2004.
Photo by Shaun Botterill/Getty Images

Below The peloton climbs the Col de Saint-Roch
during the 97th Liege-Bastogne-Liege race, Belgium,
April 24, 2011.
Photo by Bryn Lennon/Getty Images

Right More than 600 canoes crammed into a lock on
the River Spree, Berlin, on their way to
a canoeing event, July 31, 1936.
Photo by Fox Photos/Getty Images

Following pages Film Set, ridden by Frankie Dettori,
wins the Vodafone E.B.F. Maiden Stakes at Newbury
Racecourse, England, October 9, 2008.
Photo by Warren Little/Getty Images

Below De Luain Gorm, ridden by Gary Gallagher, falls at the Chair jump in The John Smiths Fox Hunters Steeplechase at Aintree racecourse, Liverpool, April 2, 2009.
Photo by Julian Finney/Getty Images

Opposite page Brazil's Ioran Etchechury tumbles during the Youth Olympics Boys 2,000m Steeplechase, Bishan Stadium, Singapore, August 18, 2010.
Photo by Adam Pretty/Getty Images

Below Indian icon Sachin Tendulkar batting against South Africa in the Cricket World Cup, Nagpur, India, March 12, 2011.
Photo by Daniel Berehulak/Getty Images

Right Tendulkar celebrates reaching his century during a World Cup match against England, Bangalore, February 27, 2011.
Photo by Indranil Mukherjee/AFP/Getty Images

Above Cross country skiers at the start of the Engadine
Ski Marathon at St Moritz, Switzerland, March 1984.
Photo by Steve Powell/Getty Images

Opposite page Kenny Roberts Jnr riding in the French
Motorcycle Grand Prix at the Paul Ricard Circuit,
Le Castellet, May 23, 1999.
Photo by Michael Cooper/Getty Images

Above Home favourite Pat Rafter celebrates victory against Britain's Tim Henman and advancing to the quarter-finals of the Australian Open Tennis Championship, Melbourne Park, January 21, 2001.
Photo by Clive Brunskill/Getty Images

Right Leeds' Andrew Dunemann is upended by Hull defenders during the Rugby League Challenge Cup Final at the Millennium Stadium, Cardiff, Wales, August 27, 2005.
Photo by Warren Little/Getty Images

Above Peter Fill of Italy skis in the Men's Downhill during the Alpine FIS Ski World Championship on the Kandahar course in Garmisch-Partenkirchen, Germany, February 12, 2011.
Photo by Clive Rose/Getty Images

Left Paul Casey of England plays out of a fairway bunker on the 16th hole during the final round of the BMW PGA Championship, Wentworth, England, May 24, 2009.
Photo by Warren Little/Getty Images

Previous pages The peloton cuts a swathe through fields of sunflowers during stage 11 of the 2009 Tour de France from Vatan to Saint-Fargeau-Ponthierry, July 15, 2009.
Photo by Jasper Juinen/Getty Images

Above Brian O'Driscoll of Ireland runs at the Australia defence during a Rugby Union International at Croke Park, Dublin, Ireland, November 15, 2009.
Photo by Stu Forster/Getty Images

Opposite page Diego Maradona takes them all on, during Argentina's 1982 World Cup Group Three match against Belgium at Camp Nou, Barcelona, Spain, June 13, 1982.
Photo by Steve Powell/Allsport

Olympics section opener
Lenny Krayzelburg of the
USA stretches next to the
Olympic rings before entering
the pool for practice prior to
the Olympic Games at the
Olympic Sports Complex
Aquatic Centre in Athens,
Greece, August 11, 2004.
*Photo by Donald Miralle/Getty
Images*

Left A female competitor in
practice for her diving event
at the Olympic Park during
the 1992 Olympic Games,
Barcelona, Spain.
*Photo by Simon Bruty/
Getty Images*

Opposite page Scott Parsons of the USA competes in the men's K-1 Class Slalom heat during the Olympic Games at the Schinias Olympic Slalom Centre, Athens, Greece, August 19, 2004.
Photo by Donald Miralle/Getty Images

Above The final of the Women's 20km Walk continues in torrential rain at the Beijing Olympics, China, August 21, 2008.
Photo by Jed Jacobsohn/Getty Images

Above and opposite page Nikita Kriukov (wearing number 4) edges Russian compatriot Alexander Panzhinskiy to claim the gold medal in the Men's Individual Sprint C Final of the Winter Olympics at Whistler Olympic Park Biathlon Stadium, Whistler, Canada, February 17, 2010.
Photo by Lars Baron/Bongarts/Getty Images

Above USA's Keith Smart (left) and Alexey Yakimenko of Russia face off in the Men's Fencing Team Sabre bronze medal match at the Athens Olympics, Greece, August 19, 2004.

Photo by Donald Miralle/Getty Images

Above left Daley Thompson flips over with glee during the pole vault event on his way to winning the Decathalon and setting a new world record at the LA Olympics, USA, August 12, 1984.
Photo by Steve Powell/Allsport

Above Brit Terry Bartlett vaults during the Men's All-Around Gymnastics competition at the Seoul Olympics, South Korea, September 24, 1988.
Photo by Pascal Rondeau/Getty Images

Left A kayak rower during early morning practice prior to the Men's K-1 class 500m semi-final at the Schinias Olympic Rowing and Canoeing Centre, Athens, Greece, August 26, 2004.
Photo by Clive Brunskill/Getty Images

Below Sonja Johnson of Australia and Ringwould Jaguar perform their Dressage Test at the Hong Kong Olympic Equestrian Venue during the Beijing Olympic Games, Sha Tin, China, August 10, 2008.
Photo by Julian Herbert/Getty Images

Above Canada's women's ice hockey team celebrate beating USA 2-0 in the final at the Vancouver Winter Olympics, Canada, February 25, 2010.
Photo by Alex Livesey/Getty Images

Right Eva Huckova of Slovakia competes in the Women's Alpine Skiing Downhill Training, in San Sicario Fraiteve, Italy, at the Winter Olympic Games, February 13, 2006.
Photo by Shaun Botterill/Getty Images

Previous pages Svetlana Radkevich of Belarus competes with Australia's Sophie Muir during the Women's Speed Skating 500m at Richmond Olympic Oval during the Vancouver Winter Olympics, Canada, February 16, 2010.
Photo by Jamie Squire/Getty Images

Opposite page Reese Hoffa of the USA competes in the Men's Shot Putt final at the National Stadium, Beijing, China, August 15, 2008.
Photo by Stu Forster/Getty Images

Above Home favourite Huo Liang performs a dive in the Men's 10m Platform FInal at the National Aquatics Center, Beijing, China, August 23, 2008.
Photo by Shaun Botterill/Getty Images

Left and below Evgeniya Polyakova, Yulia Gushchina, Yuliya Chermoshanskaya and Aleksandra Fedoriva of Russia celebrate after their victory in the Women's 4 x 100m Relay Final at the Olympic Games, Beijing, China, August 22, 2008.
Left: Photo by Al Bello/Getty Images
Below: Photo by Shaun Botterill/Getty Images

Opposite page Victor Sanyeyev of Russia on his way to the gold medal in the Men's Triple Jump at the 1972 Olympic Games, Munich, Germany.
Photo by Tony Duffy/Allsport

Above Wu Minxia of China competes in the Olympic Women's 3m Springboard final held at the National Aquatics Centre, Beijing, China, August 17, 2008.
Photo by Adam Pretty/Allsport

Above TC Dantzler of the USA (in red, foreground) and Peter Bacsi (blue) of Hungary compete in a Men's Greco-Roman 74kg qualification bout at the Beijing Olympics, China, August 13, 2008.
Photo by Clive Rose/Getty Images

Above Women archers compete in the 'National Round' (60 yards and 50 yards), won by Sybil 'Queenie' Newall of Great Britain, at the 1908 London Olympics.

Photo by Topical Press Agency/Getty Images

Top The Norwegian team in the Speed Skating Women's Team Pursuit, at the 2006 Winter Olympic Games, Turin, Italy.
Photo by Clive Rose/Getty Images

Above German gymnast Fabian Hambuechen on the horizontal bar at the Beijing Olympics, August 9, 2008.
Photo by Mike Hewitt/Getty Images

Right England's Rachel Ennis competes in the Commonwealth Games Rhythmic Gymnastics Individual Hoop Apparatus final at the Indira Gandhi Sports Complex, New Delhi, India, October 14, 2010.
Photo by: Manpreet Romana/AFP/Getty Images

Above Alexander Spitz of Germany in action before
he falls and breaks his leg during the Downhill LW2
Class at the Winter Paralympics in Nagano, Japan,
March 1, 1998.
Photo by Alex Livesey/Getty Images

Right American Bob Beamon breaking the Long Jump
world record with a leap of 8.90m at the Olympic
Games in Mexico City, Mexico, October 18, 1968.
Photo by Tony Duffy/Allsport

Above Usain Bolt of Jamaica celebrates as he approaches the line in the Men's Olympic 100m final at the National Stadium, Beijing, China, August 16, 2008. Bolt clocked a new world record time of 9.69 seconds.
Photo by Vladimir Rys/Bongarts/Getty Images

Opposite page Bolt reacts after winning gold and setting a new world record (19.30 seconds) in the Men's Olympic 200m final, August 20, 2008.
Top: Photo by Michael Steele/Getty Images
Below: Photo by Alexander Hassenstein/Bongarts/ Getty Images

Opposite page A diver spins during the 3m Springboard event at the Atlanta Olympic Games, Georgia, USA, July 28, 1996.
Photo by Stu Forster/Getty Images

Opposite page Oleksandr Bortiuk finds himself facing the wrong way in the Unified Team's sled during their run in the Four-Man Bobsleigh competition at the 1992 WInter Olympic Games, Albertville, France, February 22, 1992.
Photo by Simon Bruty/Getty Images

Following pages A man watching a ski jump competitor against the cityscape during the 1988 Winter Olympics, Calgary, Canada.
Photo by Chris Smith/Getty Images

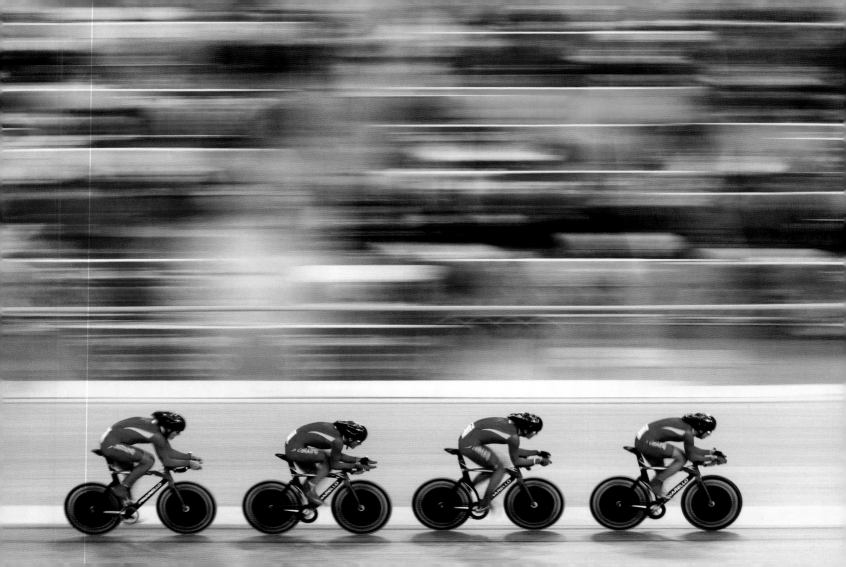

Above Olympic decathletes recover after crossing the
finish line of the 1500m Heat 2 event, Beijing, China,
August 22, 2008.
Photo by Jamie Squire/Getty Images

Opposite page Russian weightlifter Dmitriy Klokov
reacts during the Olympic final of the Men's 105kg
event, Beijing, China, August 18, 2008. Klokov went
on to win the silver medal.
Photo by Shaun Botterill/Getty Images

Olympics section final image The closing ceremony of the Olympic Games viewed from outside the 'Bird Nest' Stadium, Beijing, China, on August 24, 2008.
Photo by Al Bello/Getty Images

Right The Rue Ziffra, PA Attorney at Law Toyota driven by Mike Skinner flies over the hood of T.J. Bell's VisitPIT.com/Red Horse Racing Toyota during the NASCAR Camping World Series North Carolina Education Lottery 200, at Lowe's Motor Speedway, Concord, North Carolina, May 15, 2009.
Photo by Geoff Burke/Getty Images for NASCAR

Above Evgeni Malkin of the Pittsburgh Penguins warms
up before playing the New York Islanders at the Nassau
Coliseum, Uniondale, New York, February 16, 2009.
Photo by Jim McIsaac/Getty Images

Right Ronnie O'Sullivan of England plays a shot
against Mark Williams of Wales in the World Snooker
Championship quarter-final at the Crucible Theatre,
Sheffield, April 30, 2008.
Photo by Paul Gilham/Getty Images

Left Wayne Rooney of Manchester United scores a goal with a spectacular overhead kick during a Premier League match against Manchester City at Old Trafford stadium, Manchester, England, February 12, 2011.
Photo by Alex Livesey/Getty Images

Right Cassius Clay (later Muhammad Ali) stands over felled opponent Sonny Liston in the first round of their World Heavyweight Championship rematch, Lewiston, Maine, USA, May 25, 1965. Ali had won their first encounter, and he was awarded victory by knockout, one of the most controversial stoppage decisons in boxing history.

Photo by George Silk/Time & Life Pictures/ Getty Images

Opposite page Marc Albrighton of Aston Villa and George Elokobi of Wolves battle for the ball during a Premier League match at Villa Park, Birmingham, England, March 19, 2011.
Photo by Mike Hewitt/Getty Images

Top Maria Sharapova of Russia serves against Yung-Jan Chan of Taipei in the third round of the French Open Women's Singles at Roland Garros, Paris, France, May 28, 2011.
Photo by Clive Brunskill/Getty Images

Above Dogs racing at Romford Greyhound Stadium, Essex, England, March 24, 2011.
Photo by Jamie McDonald/Getty Images

Above Messi celebrates after scoring for Barcelona against Manchester United in the UEFA Champions League final at Wembley Stadium, London, May 28, 2011.
Photo by Lluis Gene/AFP/Getty Images

Left Argentina's Lionel Messi in action during a World Cup finals Round of Sixteen match against Mexico at Soccer City Stadium, Johannesburg, South Africa, June 27, 2010.
Photo by Mike Hewitt/FIFA via Getty Images

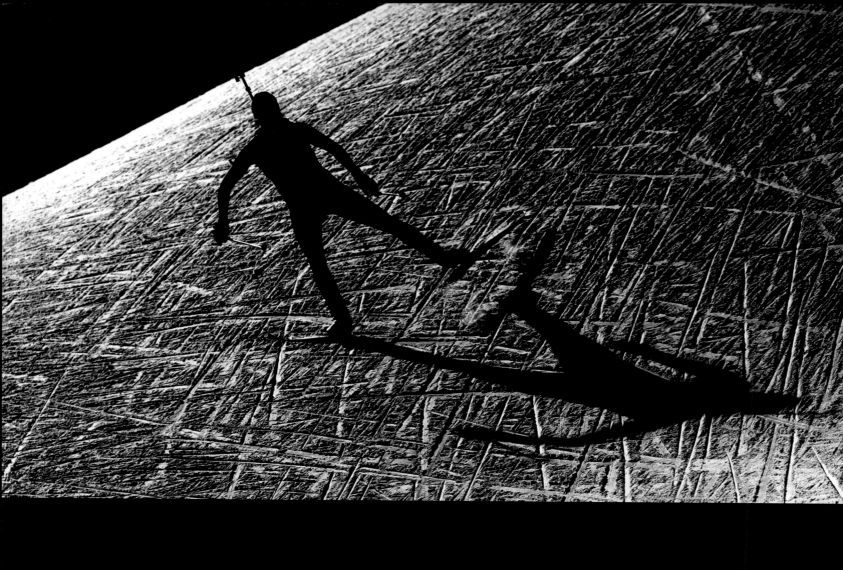

Opposite page A competitor in the Women's 4 x 6km Relay in the IBU Biathlon World Cup in Ruhpolding, Germany, January 15, 2010.
Photo by Alexander Hassenstein/Bongarts/Getty Images

Below Oiu Han of China competes in the Women's Individual Wakeboarding at Barr Al Jissah, Qantab Beach during the Asian Beach Games in Muscat, Oman, December 14, 2010.
Photo by Bryn Lennon/Getty Images

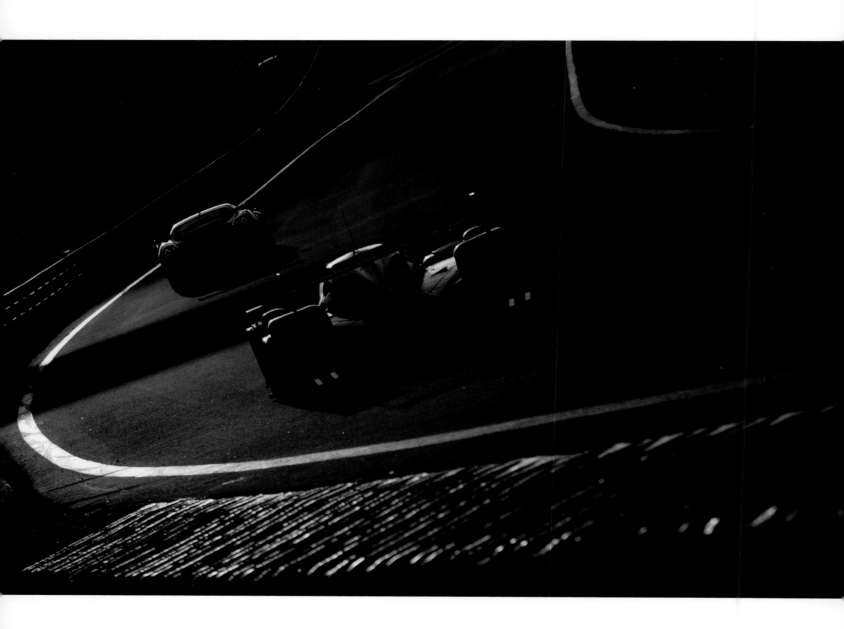

Above Cars head towards Tertre Rouge during the Le Mans 24 Hour race at the Circuit des 24 Heures du Mans, France, June 14, 2009.
Photo by Ker Robertson/Getty Images

Opposite page Garrett Johnson competes in the Women's Pole Vault during the UKA Super8 in Cardiff, Wales, June 10, 2009.
Photo by Paul Gilham/Getty Images

Following pages Festus Ezeli of the Vanderbilt
Commodores is knocked to the ground as Storm Warren
of the LSU Tigers shoots during the first round of the
SEC Men's Basketball Tournament at the Georgia Dome,
Atlanta, Georgia, March 10, 2011.
Photo by Kevin C. Cox/Getty Images

Left Patrick Mueller (left)
and goalkeeper Diego
Benaglio of Switzerland
battle for the ball with
Turkey's Arda Turan
during a UEFA Euro
2008 Group A match
at St Jakob-Park,
Basel, Switzerland,
June 11, 2008.
Photo by Alex Livesey/
Getty Images

Below Petter Solberg of Norway races the Ford Focus at the FIA World Rally Championship race in Portugal, March 21, 1999.
Photo by Mike Hewitt/Allsport

Below England's Phil 'The Power' Taylor throws at the World Darts Championship, Alexandra Palace, London, England, December 27, 2011.
Photo by Dean Mouhtaropoulos/Getty Images

Below Maria Sharapova of Russia after victory against USA's Serena Williams in the Wimbledon Lawn Tennis Championship Ladies Singles final, London, England, July 3, 2004.
Photo by Mike Hewitt/Getty Images

Opposite page Iwan Thomas flies the flag for Wales after victory in the 400m at the Commonwealth Games, Kuala Lumpur, Malaysia, September 19, 1998.
Photo by Stu Forster/Getty Images

Following pages England's Jonathan Trott dives in vain as he is run out by Simon Katich of Australia during day one of the Fifth Ashes Test Match at The Brit Oval, London, England, August 20, 2009.
Photo by Tom Shaw/Getty Images

Below Allan Donald of South Africa is run out and Australia go through to the World Cup final after a dramatic semi-final match finishes tied at Edgbaston, Birmingham, England, June 17, 1999. Australia qualify for the final after finishing higher in the SuperSix table.
Photo by Ross Kinnaird/Allsport

Opposite page Sebastien Bourdais of France in the Toro Rosso car makes a pitstop during the Spanish Formula One Grand Prix at the Circuit de Catalunya, Barcelona, Spain, April 27, 2008.
Photo by Mark Thompson/Getty Images

Left Amir Johnson of the
Radford Highlanders drives
into Larry Drew II of the
North Carolina Tar Heels
during the first round of
the NCAA Division 1 Men's
Basketball Tournament, in
North Carolina, USA,
March 19, 2009.
*Photo by Streeter Lecka/
Getty Images*

Opposite page Spaniard Rafael Nadal reacts during the US Open Men's Singles Final against Novak Djokovic of Serbia at the USTA Billie Jean King National Tennis Center, New York City, September 13, 2010.
Photo by Chris Trotman/Getty Images for USTA

Above Nadal stretches to play a backhand against Novak Djokovic of Serbia in their ATP Masters Series quarter-final match at the Foro Italico complex, Rome, Italy, May 11, 2007.
Photo by Clive Brunskill/Getty Images

Below Giant Russian Nikolai Valuev lands a left on David Haye of Britain during his unsuccessful defence of the WBA World Heavyweight title at the Nuernberger Versicherung Arena, Nuremberg, Germany, November 7, 2009.
Photo by Alex Grimm/Bongarts/Getty Images

Opposite page Konishiki, 'The Dumptruck' of Hawaii, stares down at his opponent during the first Sumo Bashai held outside Japan, at the Albert Hall, London, England, November 1991.
Photo by Chris Cole/Getty Images

Opposite page Liverpool's Steven Gerrard falls over Mark Noble of West Ham during a Premier League match at Upton Park, May 9, 2009.
Photo by Shaun Botterill/Getty Images

Above Tom Croft of England scores a try against Scotland at Twickenham Stadium, March 13, 2011.
Photo by David Rogers/Getty Images

Opposite page Jessica Ennis of Great Britain competes in the Women's Heptathlon (High Jump) during the IAAF World Athletics Championship at the Olympic Stadium, Berlin, Germany, August 15, 2009.

Photo by Michael Steele/Getty Images

Below Mikhail Koudinov of New Zealand competes in the parallel bars during the Artistic Gymnastics World Championship at O2 Arena, London, England, October 13, 2009.

Photo by Clive Rose/Getty Images

Following pages Rory McIlroy of Northern Ireland tees off on the tenth hole in the third round of the 111th US Open, at Congressional Country Club, Bethesda, Maryland, June 18, 2011.
Photo by David Cannon/Getty Images

Below The Corvette Racing Chevrolet Corvette C6-R, driven by Johnny O'Connell, in practice for the American Le Mans Series Petit Le Mans at Road Atlanta, Braselton, Georgia, USA, September 29, 2006.
Photo by Darrell Ingham/Getty Images

Right Austria's Michaela Kirchgasser (left) and Anemone Marmottan of France race in the Nations Team Event at the Alpine FIS Ski World Championship, Garmisch-Partenkirchen, Germany, February 16, 2011.
Photo by Clive Mason/Getty Images

Above Spaniard Jaime Alguersuari of Scuderia Toro
Rosso retires from the Hungarian Formula One Grand
Prix at the Hungaroring, Budapest, August 1, 2010.
Photo by Paul Gilham/Getty Images

Opposite page Filipino boxing legend Manny Pacquiao
KOs Ricky Hatton of England in the second round of
their Junior Welterweight title fight at the MGM Grand
Garden Arena, Las Vegas, Nevada, USA, May 2, 2009.
Photo by Al Bello/Getty Images

Previous pages Kim Clijsters of Belgium waits to return
serve in her Australian Open semi-final match against
Russian Vera Zvonareva, Melbourne Park, Melbourne,
January 27, 2011.
Photo by Julian Finney/Getty Images

Left Filippo Inzaghi of AC Milan celebrates scoring the first goal in the UEFA Champions League final against Liverpool at the Olympic Stadium, Athens, Greece, May 23, 2007.
Photo by Laurence Griffiths/Getty Images

Above Tim Thomas of the Boston Bruins can't stop a shot from Vancouver Canucks' Maxim Lapierre during Game Five of the NHL Stanley Cup finals at Rogers Arena, Vancouver, Canada, June 10, 2011.
Photo by Jeff Vinnick/NHL via Getty Images

Opposite page Pier Oliver Cote of Canada reacts after defeating Aris Ambriz in a super lightweight fight at MGM Grand Garden Arena, Las Vegas, Nevada, USA, May 7, 2011.
Photo by Chris Trotman/Getty Images

Above Rio Ferdinand of Manchester United celebrates his team's 6-5 penalty shootout victory in the UEFA Champions League final versus Chelsea at the Luzhniki Stadium, Moscow, Russia, May 21, 2008.
Photo by Shaun Botterill/Getty Images

Above Matt Prior and captain Andrew Strauss (right) of
England celebrate victory in The Ashes series against
Australia at Sydney Cricket Ground, Sydney, Australia,
January 7, 2011.
Photo by Tom Shaw/Getty Images

Opposite page Jonathan Casillas of the New Orleans Saints
enjoys a confetti storm after the Saints defeat the Minnesota
Vikings in the NFC Championship Game at the Louisiana
Superdome, New Orleans, USA, January 24, 2010.
Photo by Ronald Martinez/Getty Images

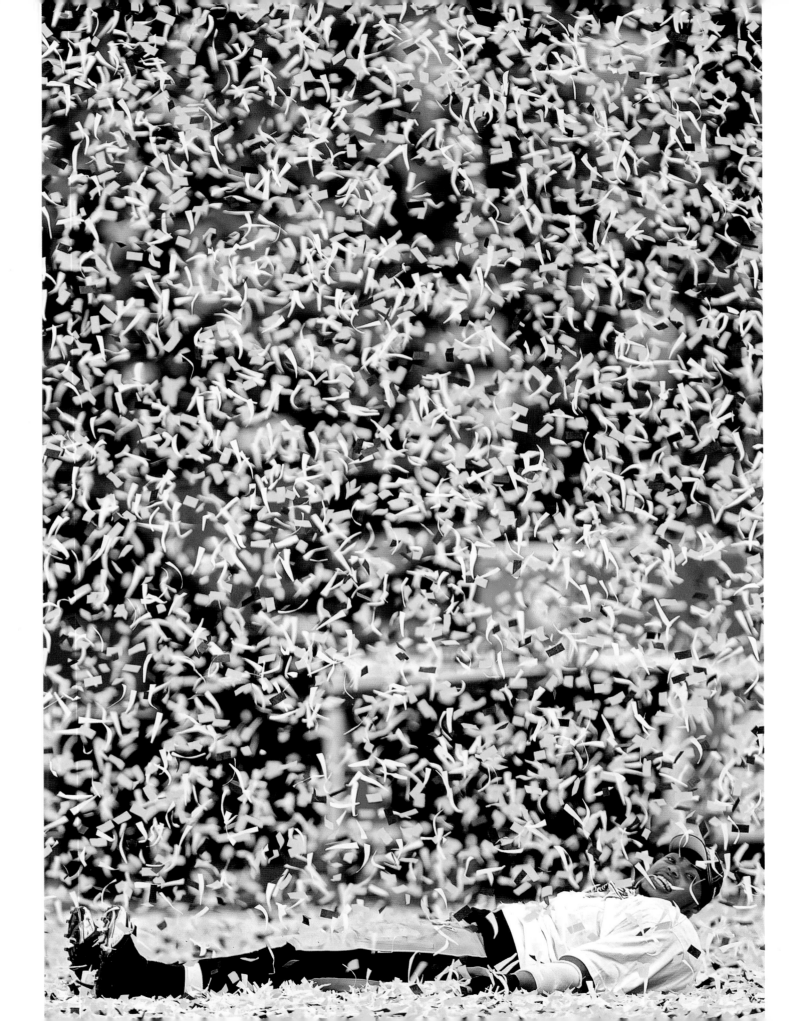

Published by Vision Sports Publishing in 2011

Vision Sports Publishing
19-23 High Street
Kingston upon Thames
Surrey
KT1 1LL

www.visionsp.co.uk

ISBN: 978-1-907637-34-6

All photography supplied by Getty Images

gettyimages®

www.gettyimages.com

Editor: Justyn Barnes
Design: Neal Cobourne
Picture research: Ker Robertson
Commissioning editor: Rick Mayston

Printed in Slovakia by Niografia
A CIP Catalogue record for this book is available from the British Library